Original title:
Tropical Winds

Copyright © 2025 Creative Arts Management OÜ
All rights reserved.

Author: Dorian Ashford
ISBN HARDBACK: 978-1-80581-497-9
ISBN PAPERBACK: 978-1-80581-024-7
ISBN EBOOK: 978-1-80581-497-9

An Afternoon in Paradise

The sun's out, my friend, oh what a sight,
A coconut hat, feels just right.
The palm trees dance, they wiggle and sway,
I'm chasing my drink, it's gonna get away!

With sand in my shoes, I start to groove,
I trip on a crab, oh what a move!
The seagulls squawk, they think they can sing,
But my beach ball's got a better fling!

Driftwood Dreams and Sunbeams

A piece of driftwood lies on the shore,
I swear it's a surfboard, oh what a score!
But as I hop on, it starts to float,
I grab a sea turtle, let's set the boat!

Sunbeams tickle my silly little nose,
I start to dance, in flip-flops and toes.
The beach chairs cheer, they rock and roll,
As I fall in the sand, that's my main goal!

Where the Blue Waves Call

The ocean's calling, with a bubbly cheer,
I try to surf, but whoops, I just steer.
The waves wash over, they laugh with glee,
I wipe out again, oh look, there's a bee!

Seagulls are giggling, what a fine show,
They steal my fries, as if they know!
The surfboard floats like a feathered kite,
While I flounder around, what a comical sight!

Paradise in the Air

Up in the hammock, so cozy and bright,
I dream of coconuts, taking a bite.
But a squirrel leaps in, steals my sweet snack,
I yell, "Come back here!" as he scurries back!

The breeze starts to tickle, oh what a tease,
I scatter my chips, now they're caught in the trees!
With a drink in my hand and laughter to share,
I'm the king of this chaos, paradise in the air!

Where the Horizon Meets the Breeze

The parrot squawks with flair,
While seagulls dive with grace,
I tripped on my beach chair,
Now sand's in every place!

A crab wore my lost flip-flop,
He strutted with such pride,
As I laughed and nearly dropped,
This whirlwind of a ride!

Sunlit Hues of the Shore

With sunscreen on my nose,
I dance like no one's there,
The ocean waves just pose,
And giggle at my flair.

A dolphin jumped to see,
What chaos I could bring,
He snorted with pure glee,
I guess I'm quite the thing!

The Embrace of Salt and Sea

A wave crashed down with might,
It knocked me off my feet,
I shouted, "What a sight!"
As sand danced to the beat.

The wind threw my hat high,
It landed on a tree,
The monkeys laughed nearby,
Envying my spree!

Echoes from the Isle's Edge

The coconut fell with a thud,
I hid, avoiding doom,
As it rolled through the mud,
And filled my beachy room.

Friendship bracelets on my wrist,
I wove them in a rush,
But found a jellyfish,
That gave my fingers a hush!

The Allure of Warm Sands

The sun shines bright, it laughs and plays,
While sandcastles crumble in funny ways.
A flip-flop flies, is it a bird?
Oh wait, it's my shoe! This is absurd!

With each wave's crash, a giggle's born,
Seagulls squawk, quite the comical horn.
Beach balls bounce, oh what a sight,
And sunscreen fights the battle of white!

Canvas of Nature's Palette

Blue skies above, in a paintbox spread,
With colors so bright, they dance in my head.
A palm tree sways, doing a jig,
While I laugh hard at a flamingo's wig!

Breezes chuckle as they tickle the grass,
While coconuts drop with a thud, oh alas!
Nature's canvas, a funny display,
Where the clouds wear hats in a silly way!

Journey through a Lush Paradise

A parrot squawks, "Let's have some fun!"
As I trip over vines, oh what a run!
Butterflies flutter, they giggle and zoom,
While I wander clueless, lost in the bloom!

Every turn shows a quirky little sight,
Monkeys throw coconuts, oh what a fright!
In this lush maze, laughter echoes wide,
As I dance with hedgehogs, friends by my side!

The Invitation of the Glistening Coast

The sea sparkles, inviting and bright,
"Come splash with us," it calls with delight.
A crab in a tux, all dressed for the dance,
Waves of laughter—oh, give it a chance!

Sandy feet shuffle in a goofy parade,
As seaweed wigs sway, oh what a charade!
The shoreline beckons with giggles galore,
And we run with joy, who could ask for more?

Whispers of the Palms

The palms are gossiping, oh what a scene,
They talk of coconuts and monkeys, so keen.
With each rustle and sway, they giggle and tease,
While sunbathers wonder about their expertise.

A parrot joins in, all feathers and flair,
Claiming he's got the juiciest stare.
The breeze tickles leaves, causes fitful delight,
While sunburned tourists dance late into night.

Dance of the Gentle Breezes

The breezes waltz on a hot summer day,
Making palm fronds sway in a silly ballet.
A flip-flop flies off in a gust with a cheer,
As nearby tourists spill drinks, full of beer!

A crab scuttles by, with a tap in his step,
Trying to catch the rhythm, oh what a prep!
He joins the festivities, a crustacean so bold,
As the dance floor erupts in stories retold.

Breath of the Ocean's Serenade

The sea hums a tune, with bubbles that pop,
While beach balls are juggled, they never do stop.
A dolphin dives in, donning sunglasses so bright,
A flip and a twist, what a comical sight!

Seagulls squawk loudly, they want in the mix,
They steal from the picnics, those crafty old tricks.
As children chase waves, and the tides pull away,
The ocean's soft laugh makes for a great play.

Echoes Through the Canopy

In the tree tops high, there's a party so grand,
With monkeys swinging to a percussion band.
The leaves start to rustle, a jubilant fuss,
While squirrels throw acorns, just making a fuss!

The echoes of laughter flow down through the trees,
A soundscape of joy, riding every light breeze.
With a splash in the creek, and a jump on the ground,
The forest is buzzing, with merriment found.

Shoreline Secrets at Dusk

The crabs all dance with glee,
In shadows, they're hard to see.
They scuttle left, they scuttle right,
In the fading whispers of light.

Seashells gossip out of turn,
Each one has a tale to learn.
As the sun kisses the bay,
It laughs, then slowly slips away.

The seagulls play their goofy tricks,
Stealing fries, oh what a fix!
With every splash, a squeaky sound,
The shoreline secrets all around.

As the stars begin to gleam,
I join the crabs in their dream.
Together we waltz, in our array,
On the edge where night meets day.

The Symphony of the Ocean's Caress

The waves come in with a whoosh,
Like a band that starts to swoosh.
Each splash is a note, full of cheer,
Ocean's choir carries near.

Seashells tap their tiny feet,
Joining in with a rhythmic beat.
A fish jumps up with a flip,
Making sure it's part of the trip.

A dolphin prances with a grin,
As if to say, "Let the fun begin!"
The fish all giggle and swirl about,
In this playful aquatic rout.

The sun bows down, clap-clap-clap,
As the ocean waves, a funny lap.
In this concert, we all partake,
With laughter shared in every break.

Beneath a Canopy of Leaves

Under leaves that whisper tales,
A squirrel plans nutty fails.
He takes a leap, misses his aim,
Falling down, now what a shame!

The monkeys play a game of tag,
A swinging world, with a loud brag.
They tumble down, give a shout,
Stick to trees, what a route!

With flowers bright, they twist and sway,
In the breeze, they laugh and play.
A toucan mocks with a funny call,
"Catch me if you can, or not at all!"

Beneath this roof, let's all embrace,
Nature's joy, a silly space.
In every nook, a giggle's found,
Beneath the leaves, we laugh around.

Dance of the Feathery Fronds

The palm trees sway like they can groove,
In the sun, they start to move.
With every gust, their dance begins,
A foxtrot led by cheeky winds.

Coconuts roll, it's a bumpy ride,
While parrots squawk, they can't hide.
One slips down and starts to spin,
Laughing hard, he joins the din.

The fronds do twist, a wiggly feat,
As laughter sweeps through every street.
The sun gets low, a dazzling show,
With dancing leaves, they steal the glow.

Underneath this feather dance,
The world joyfully takes a chance.
In a whirligig of life and fun,
Nature smiles at everyone.

Once Upon a Whispered Voyage

Upon a ship made of bright cheese,
Sailed the captain with wobbly knees.
He chased the sun, in a silly dance,
Until a seagull stole his pants.

The fish wore hats, and danced a jig,
While the crew laughed, and did a pig.
With every gust, they'd spin and sway,
Chasing their hats that flew away.

A parrot squawked, 'We're lost, I fear!'
But the crew just toasted with pirate cheer.
They toasted to ham and cheesy bread,
As the ship sailed on, hilariously led.

So if you seek adventure true,
Just hop on a cheese boat, and join the crew.
For laughter echoes on every shore,
Where the fanciful tales of cheese are more!

Chasing Dreams in the Breeze

In a hammock hung between two trees,
Lay a cat, swaying with the breeze.
He dreamt of fish in fancy hats,
While plotting revenge on the dancing rats.

The sunbeam tickled his furry toes,
While below, the ants played tag in rows.
The more he imagined, the more he sat,
Until a sparrow stole his favorite mat.

With a stretch and a lazy yawn,
He chased that bird at the crack of dawn.
But tripped on a leaf, right on his nose,
And landed hard, right next to the toes.

Yet laughter rang through the sunny day,
As he rolled around, in a goofy way.
For in this world of silly dreams,
Even the cats dance with laughable schemes!

Breezy Tales of the Tropics

A crab wore shades and danced on the sand,
With a swing that no one could quite understand.
He balanced a coconut on his head,
While telling a tale that left all undead.

The dolphins giggled, swimming near,
As the crab sang softly, 'Life's a cheer!'
With every splash, he twirled around,
In a world where laughter could always be found.

A fruit fly joined in with a zestful spin,
And suddenly, the sea became a win.
They had a beach party, with seashells as plates,
While the jellyfish cheered and even threw crates.

The sun set low, painting skies so bright,
The crab crawled home, what a sight!
With dreams of dance and fruit-filled pies,
In this kooky land, where fun never dies!

Fragrance of the Exotically Wild

In a garden where fruits danced so spry,
A silly monkey swung, oh my, oh my!
With a banana phone, he'd prank all day,
Saying, 'Can you hear me? No, I'm not a buffet!'

The flowers giggled at the monkey's schemes,
As he slipped on petals, lost in dreams.
Each flower scented with a humorous grin,
And soon the whole garden burst out in spin.

Bees started buzzing in sync with the beat,
As the monkey jived on his wobbly feet.
With a splash of juice from a pineapple spree,
He declared, 'This party is just for me!'

So in this wild and colorful place,
Where every laugh brings a smile to your face,
The monkey reigns with his fruity throne,
A jester of joy, forever alone!

Ethereal Echoes of the Dusk

Under the sky where coconuts sway,
Parrots squawk jokes that just won't decay.
A crab in a tux, he struts down the sand,
While flip-flops dance like they've made a new plan.

The stars start to giggle, the moon rolls its eyes,
As dancers in grass skirts perform their surprise.
A hammock is swaying, the drinks overflow,
Even the palm trees are putting on a show.

Umbrellas are twirling, drinks spill on the ground,
And flip-flops are giggling without making a sound.
The sunset is blushing, the sea takes a dive,
Where laughs flow like waves, and all feel alive.

So come take a seat, let the laughter flow,
In this place full of joy, where silly winds blow.
With shadows that dance and the breeze that will tease,
Life's a big laugh on the soft, sandy breeze.

Dances of Color on a Canvas of Blue

There's a parrot named Pete, with a colorful chat,
He tells all the secrets of the beach and the brat.
With guavas and laughter, a feast out of tune,
While jellyfish waltz under a glittering moon.

Palm leaves are rustling like they're making a bet,
That crabs can outdance all their fellow bay pets.
A surfboard is giggling, riding high on a wave,
While the sun slips away, mischief it gave.

The piña coladas spin tales of delight,
As the beach balls juggle in a slippery flight.
With laughter and cheer, the sky bursts with hues,
In this vibrant fiesta of blues and of views.

So join in the fun, let your worries take flight,
On this canvas of color where spirits unite.
With the ocean's embrace and the laughter that flows,
You'll find something funny in how the wind blows.

Floating with the Ailsa's Embrace

A buoy with a grin bobs along in the breeze,
The jellybeans watch as they float with such ease.
While fish wear pajamas, it's quite the affair,
And even the seaweed is flipping its hair.

The waves whisper jokes to the nearby boats,
Each one is a gem, just like bright, little notes.
With dolphins all giggling and splashing about,
They're planning a party, there's never a doubt.

In the hammock of laughter that sways to the beat,
Crabs are having a hoedown with colorful feet.
The sun's got a wink, as it peeks though the pines,
Where humor and joy mix like the best of wines.

So float in the merriment, let worries all cease,
Find joy in the rhythm, the waves bring you peace.
With jigs and with jests, let the evening take shape,
As the horizon chuckles and the sea takes a cape.

A Breath of Paradise's Night

The night wears a crown of bright, twinkling light,
While lizards tell tales of their favorite flight.
A turtle named Ted wears a hat with a flair,
He dances the cha-cha while lounging in air.

The sand turns to velvet, the stars start to cheer,
With a twist of the moon, all the shadows appear.
Cocktails are mingling, umbrellas in flight,
As the fireflies sparkle, revealing their delight.

With laughter and lullabies drifting from beaches,
The night gasps for joy as the cool wind beseeches.
Bright lanterns are swaying, and so is the joy,
With the rhythm of life that no one can annoy.

So gather your friends for a night full of glee,
In this breath of enchantment, you might hear a plea.
To dance and to giggle, till the dawn starts to glow,
On this quirky adventure, where joy's always flow.

A Warm Embrace from Afar

The breeze decided it was bold,
To ruffle hair and shake the mold.
A parrot squawks, a rubber chicken,
And all the cats start crazy kickin'.

Lemonade spills from laughter's cup,
A hula hoop won't spin on up.
Sandcastle dreams begin to waver,
As surfboards dance like cotton paper.

The Spirit of Life's Tides

Waves roll in with a playful tease,
As crabs scuttle with puzzled knees.
The fish are laughing, swimming fast,
While dolphins cheer, no need to gasp.

Shells hum tunes of ancient lore,
Wink as waves crash on the shore.
Seagulls argue 'bout who's the best,
While beach towels fight for space to rest.

Twilight Stories beneath the Stars

Under stars that wink and twirl,
Signaling to every clam and girl.
A firefly performs a show,
While glowworms dance, and crickets crow.

Marshmallows roast with snickering glee,
Watch out for s'mores that run free!
The moon just chuckles at our plight,
As shadows play in the silver light.

Heaven's Breath in Salt and Light

Saltwater kisses the sun-soaked fun,
But flip-flops flee and can't be won.
A seagull swoops with hopeful glee,
　Stealing fries, 'Oh woe is me!'

Pineapples wearing silly hats,
Try to roll, but fall like brats.
Each gust brings giggles, laughter's flight,
As beach balls bounce in pure delight.

Fluttering Leaves After Rain

Puddles form and splashes gleam,
Leaves dance wildly in a dream.
I slip and slide, a clumsy sprite,
In a battle with the rain's delight.

Jackets flutter, umbrellas flip,
We form a ragtag sailing ship.
Laughter echoes through the trees,
As nature plays its tricks with ease.

Rain boots squishing, socks a mess,
We laugh so hard, we can't suppress.
Water's embrace, a slippery thrill,
With every step, a joyous spill.

When sunshine breaks, the laughter stays,
A secret pact, in soggy ways.
We'll brave the clouds for more mayhem,
In puddles found, life's a gem!

Driftwood Stories in Soft Light

A stick of wood, so rough and worn,
Tells tales of storms and breezes born.
Sandy shores become our stage,
As I act out a driftwood page.

Crabs scuttle like they own the place,
While seagulls laugh, no hint of grace.
A fish appears, I tell it jokes,
About the waves and silly folks.

The sun dips low, a golden hue,
I share my stories with the crew.
A driftwood throne, a grand old seat,
As tides roll in, we find our beat.

With every wave, a chuckle near,
The ocean's voice, all we can hear.
In twilight's glow, driftwood does sway,
As laughter bids the night to stay.

The Call of Sandy Shores

Seashells whisper, secrets true,
Calling out for me and you.
Footprints giggle in the sand,
Dancing in a merry band.

Kites take flight, like crazy birds,
While we tell tales, silly words.
A sandcastle with a moat so wide,
Becomes the fortress of our pride.

Sunscreen smudged upon our nose,
We wave at waves, what fun it shows.
The beach ball flies, a graceful arc,
Our laughter echoes, a joyful spark.

As sunset paints the sky so bright,
We chase the dusk, oh what a sight.
Sandy shores, forever roam,
In silly dreams, we find our home.

Melodies of the Wind-kissed Night

Stars twinkle, a cheeky show,
As breezes dance, and crickets crow.
The night sings soft, a funny tune,
Under the gaze of a round, bright moon.

Glowing fireflies span the air,
A lantern parade, without a care.
We sway to tunes of things unseen,
With giggling shadows all around, keen.

A burp from trees, a giggling sprout,
Nature's laughter, no room for doubt.
Each rustle's a whisper, a playful jest,
As dreams wander, we give it our best.

With blankets spread, we share our dreams,
The night giggles, or so it seems.
In this melody of glee and light,
We dance and play through endless night.

Caress of the Golden Sunsets

Golden rays paint the skies bright,
While piña coladas take flight.
Seagulls dancing on the beach,
Stealing fries within their reach.

Flip-flops squeak with every step,
As sunburned tourists adept.
Chasing crabs that scuttle fast,
While sandcastles melt, unsurpassed.

Palm trees sway, doing their dance,
As beach balls bounce, they take a chance.
But sunhats blow away with glee,
Leaving folks with sandy debris.

Evenings bring a fiery glow,
While laughter fills the air below.
With cocktails raised, we sing and cheer,
A sunset party, oh so near!

A Breeze Among the Blossoms

Flowers bloom in vibrant hues,
As bees buzz wildly, spreading news.
A gentle gust pulls at my clothes,
And tickles noses, oh how it goes!

Mangoes drop with thuds so loud,
While squirrels scurry, oh so proud.
With every twist of swaying trees,
Life dances on a sweet summer breeze.

Sun hats fly like kites in the sky,
As folks look up, with a puzzled why.
Neighbors laugh, their hats all spun,
Chasing them like a comical run.

The air is sweet with fragrant air,
As kids chase butterflies without a care.
In this floral folly, hearts align,
Under the warmth, everything's finc!

Shadow Play of the Trade Winds

In the shadows, we play and hide,
As breezes tease with a cheeky ride.
Tanned tourists strut, feeling so grand,
With ice cream cones all close at hand.

Umbrellas flip like upside-down boats,
While beach bum talks get our votes.
Chasin' shadows, we dash and scoot,
As laughter echoes, oh what a hoot!

The sun grins down, a mischievous face,
As we lose ourselves in this jovial place.
Sandy footprints lead a silly race,
With ones covered from head to base.

Jellyfish bouncy, like rubbery toys,
While kids giggle, making noise.
In this shadow play of breezy jest,
Life's a joke; we're simply blessed!

Tides and Whispers of Serenity

Waves wash in, a playful tease,
Whispers of laughter ride the breeze.
Gentle tides tickle our toes,
Bubbles burst, as mischief grows.

A hermit crab takes a stroll,
In his shell, he plays the role.
Turtles glide; the fish all swirl,
In this watery dance, we twirl.

The sun plays peek-a-boo at dusk,
While we share secrets, it's a must.
Seashells rattle, like maracas bright,
As we shimmy in the fading light.

Each wave a chuckle, each foam a sigh,
As we lay back and let time fly.
With smiles wide and hearts set free,
In this paradise, we just be!

Fluttering Petals in the Breeze

Petals dance with giggly zeal,
A sneaky breeze, a floral wheel.
They toss and twirl in silly flight,
Playing tag with a bee in sight.

Down they tumble, all in a heap,
They whisper secrets, a petal creep.
Laughing loudly, they plot a prank,
To tickle a nose by the garden tank.

A butterfly joins in for fun,
Spinning 'round like a shot out of a gun.
They roll and flutter, no time to pause,
Winking at daisies with cheeky jaws.

Together they giggle, a flowery squad,
Making a ruckus, they'll not be shod.
With each gentle push of the breezy tune,
The garden watches, a flowered cartoon.

Murmurs of the Swaying Grass

In fields where giggles softly sway,
The grass whispers jokes, come out and play.
Each blade a comedian, sharp and spry,
Tickling toes that just wander by.

They wiggle and waggle, what a sight!
Grass-blades giggle with all their might.
With every gust, they chuckle and hum,
Inviting the cows to join in the fun.

A rabbit hops in, ears flopped in glee,
Joining the laughter, feeling so free.
"Why did the corn cross the road?" they ask,
"To see the salad and complete the task!"

As the sun dips low, the jokes still hiss,
The swaying grass sings tunes of bliss.
A meadow of laughter, absurd and bright,
Where grass is the punchline, evening's light.

Laughter of Waters and Winds

A babbling brook with a splashy grin,
Gurgling happily, the fun begins.
It tumbles and frolics, a watery spree,
"Catch me if you can!" says he with glee.

The winds join in, with a whoosh and a swirl,
They tickle the waves, give laughter a whirl.
"Careful!" they tease, "You might just spill,
Your drink is not safe! We're here for the thrill!"

The fish dance about, their fins all aflutter,
They leap with joy, making the water stutter.
"Water ballet!" they shout as they dive,
In the laughter of currents, they come alive.

As day turns to dusk, the waters do sigh,
They giggle and sparkle beneath the sky.
With whispers of mirth that never grow old,
They share their secrets, both gleeful and bold.

Echoes of the Sunlit Shore

On golden sands with laughter bright,
Waves crash and giggle, pure delight.
They tickle the toes of kids at play,
With splashes of joy, they shout, "Hooray!"

Seagulls join in with a cheeky shriek,
"Sandcastles crumbling! Ha, what a leak!"
Their wings flap wildly, a swooping mess,
As they steal snacks in a feathery quest.

The sun rolls downward, a golden coin,
Children laugh, their joy they enjoin.
"Race you to the sea!" the bravest declare,
As they dash and tumble, without a care.

With each echoing wave comes a new silly tale,
As shells wear their laughter like a grand veil.
On the sunlit shore, where giggles abound,
The echoes of fun and frolic resound.

The Ethereal Drift of the Breeze

In the tropics, a sigh floats by,
It tickles my nose, oh my, oh my!
A parrot squawks, thinks he can sing,
While I'm here searching for my lost fling.

Fluffy clouds dance and prance,
As if they've found a costume romance.
A squirrel tries to steal a coconut hat,
I'll join him if he picks up the spat!

Palm trees sway in a comical groove,
Even the crabs have got some sweet moves.
With each gust, laughter fills the day,
Tangled in leaves, I might just stay!

So let the breeze do its giggly flit,
For today's a party, I won't throw a fit!
I'll sip on my drink, with a silly grin,
As life's merry pranks swirl gently in spin.

Songs of Color in the Sky

Look up! Oh dear, what a sight to see,
A flamingo's flair might just be key!
Each bird, a brush, with colors so bright,
Makes the sky giggle with pure delight.

Why are the clouds wearing such funny hats?
Did they lose a bet with chubby little bats?
A rainbow stretches, perfect and grand,
While a seagull takes selfies, isn't that just bland?

Below, the kids run, chasing their dreams,
While a dog on a surfboard plots funny schemes.
Every breeze brings whispers of cheer,
As the sun dances, it's quite the sphere!

So let's raise a toast to this colorful show,
To the antics of nature, ready? Here we go!
With laughter and joy, let the days extend,
For life's a paper airplane, let's ascend!

Where the Sun Meets the Ocean's Edge

At dawn, the sun wears a golden crown,
While waves play tag with a sleepy town.
A crab in a tux makes quite a scene,
Dancing his jig, he thinks he's serene.

Not far off, a surfer wipes out with flair,
Splashing onlookers, who gasp and stare.
As gulls squabble over a forgotten chip,
We chuckle at nature's own quirky script.

Where sand meets water, giggles abound,
With flip-flops flying and laughter unbound.
A sandcastle leans under an artist's touch,
Crumbling away, it was fun, not much!

So let's savor each moment, make it grand,
With sun on our faces and laughter at hand.
In this seaside comedy, we'll stick together,
Creating such memories that none could measure!

An Invitation from the Southerly Breeze

Hello there, it's me, the playful air,
Want to join me in a prancing affair?
With a wiggle and giggle, I'll sweep you away,
To where flip-flops giggle and sunbeams play.

I swirl past the flowers, they nod in delight,
While the sun shouts, "Hey! Let's keep it bright!"
Laughter erupts from a nearby gazelle,
As I tickle his ears—oh, this is swell!

Grab your drink, come dance on the shore,
Jump with excitement, let's create some more!
Each gust tells stories that squeak and squall,
Inviting the world to a goofy free-for-all.

So let's ride together on this joyful spree,
With a sprinkle of magic, just you and me.
From mountains to valleys, wherever we roam,
Embrace the silliness, we'll always feel home!

Surprising Colors of the Evening

The sky yells orange, like a fruit surprise,
Lemons and limes twinkling in the skies.
A pink flamingo in a purple hat,
Sipping coconut drinks next to a cat.

Laughing waves tumble, a raucous crowd,
Umbrellas giggle, all wearing a shroud.
A duck in sunglasses struts by with flair,
While jellyfish do the wobbly air.

The clouds are like candy, fluffy and sweet,
While the sun plays peekaboo, quick on its feet.
Palm trees are swaying, a dance-off in sight,
As mangoes roll by, just stealing the light.

Night falls with sparkles, a confetti show,
Every star winks with mischief below.
The breeze whispers secrets, tickling the toes,
In this colorful evening, anything goes!

Shadows Dancing on the Shore

The shadows wiggle with quirky delight,
Doing the cha-cha by the pale moonlight.
A crab wearing sneakers shuffles with glee,
While fish in top hats groove by the sea.

The sand casts laughter, a joke on the tide,
As footprints do the limbo, side to side.
A seagull in heels chirps a silly tune,
Pulling starfish along, 'neath the silver moon.

The beachball is bouncing, just begging to play,
While seaweed waltzes, in a breezy ballet.
The laughter of shells echoes bright on the bay,
As shadows kick up and dance the night away!

With a twist and a twirl, the dark starts to blend,
A comical chaos, where giggles don't end.
In this shadowy jamboree, join in the fun,
Where laughter and whispers go on till the sun.

Where Day Meets Night

The sun yawns loudly, stretching the sky,
While crickets jump up, and the parrot just sighs.
A coconut rolls, like a cheeky old friend,
As the seagulls plot mischief, around every bend.

The horizon blushes, with colors so bright,
As bananas don tuxes for a grand twilight.
A turtle with party hats joins the parade,
While the breeze tosses confetti, like it's been made.

Stars poke their heads, just to peek at the scene,
While the moon plays a tune on a silver screen.
The day waves goodbye, with a wink and a laugh,
As the night takes the stage, like a silly giraffe.

With a chuckle and jiggle, the moon lets it flow,
As laughter and chatter start stealing the show.
In this playful moment, evening takes flight,
Where giggles and dreams dance together at night!

Sails Filled with Light

The boat is a sandwich, on waters so blue,
With jellyfish jam and sun on the crew.
A seagull's the captain, loud as a drum,
While dolphins throw parties, oh what a fun!

Sails whisper secrets, of faraway lands,
As turtles in tuxedos make intricate plans.
The breeze tugs the ropes, like a mischievous kid,
Playing tag with the waves, giggling as they hid.

With pineapple flags flying high in the sky,
A parade of sea creatures drifts boldly by.
The ocean's a circus, a flip and a dive,
Where laughter and bubbles twirl quick and alive.

As the sun dips down, igniting the sea,
The night dons her jewels, all sparkly and free.
With each wave that passes, a joke's in the air,
In this buoyant adventure, there's laughter to share!

Secrets Carried by the Wind

A feather floats with laughter high,
It tickles toucans as they fly.
The gossip spreads from tree to tree,
A parrot squawks, "Come laugh with me!"

Mangoes tumble, a surprise parade,
Pineapples giggle, dressed in jade.
A coconut wiggles, drinks in hand,
"I'm the life of this merry band!"

The breeze plays tricks, so sly and fast,
It lifts your hat; it's quite the blast!
As laughter dances upon the shore,
We chase the sand, forever more!

So when you hear those rustles loud,
Just know it's not a ghostly crowd.
The secrets swirl, a playful spin,
In every gust, joy lies within!

The Breath of Distant Shores

A ship sails by with silly sails,
And giggles echo through the gales.
A sea turtle tries to sing along,
But only gurgles come out strong!

Seagulls strut with fancy feet,
Competing for the best fish treat.
While dolphins dance like stars in night,
They flip and splash, what a sight!

The waves whisper secrets, but we can't hear,
Because the surf's just too loud, oh dear!
Yet in their foam, do see the grins,
For every splash, another begins.

Breezes tease with salty air,
They tango with the sun's warm glare.
Every gust a comic play,
In this grand show, we laugh away!

Whispers among the Palms

The palms are gossipers, don't you know?
With rustling leaves, they put on a show.
In shadows cool, they snicker along,
As monkeys come skipping, all smiles and song.

There's a sloth who thinks he's quite the star,
Takes hours to move just a few feet far.
While toucans laugh with their beak-shaped grins,
They know the slowpoke never wins!

Lizards dart in a flash of green,
Playing tag, what a crazy scene!
A sudden breeze creates a fun flurry,
As critters scurry in a merry hurry.

So next time you stroll where the palm trees sway,
Listen close; there's much to say.
For every whisper you happen to catch,
Is a tale or joke, a delightful match!

Embracing the Electric Sunset

The sky lights up, a rainbow might,
As day transforms to giggling night.
Fireflies blink like silly stars,
In an electric dance that's truly ours.

Crickets chirp a melody loud,
While frogs hold court, feeling proud.
Each croak a note, oh what a tune,
As laughter leaps beneath the moon!

The waves clap hands on the sandy shore,
Cheering the colors, begging for more.
As the sun dips low, it's quite the game,
Every hue whispers a silly name!

So let's embrace this vibrant end,
With every nature buddy, our friend.
In the glow of dusk, let's all partake,
In laughter's light, we joyously wake!

A Voyage with the Wind's Embrace

On a raft made of marshmallows,
I sailed past a crab with a hat.
He waved at the waves in pajamas,
As I giggled and patted my cat.

The waves danced like clowns in a show,
While dolphins wore shades, oh so bright.
They splashed me with goldfish confetti,
Saying, "Hey, join the silliness tonight!"

My compass was lost to a parrot,
Who squawked out the tune of a jest.
With each twist and turn of the sea,
I laughed till my heart was a fest!

So here's to the trip that we take,
With beagles and bugle bands, too.
May every wave tickle our toes,
And every breeze lead to a clue!

Mirage of the Exotic Isle

On an isle where the coconuts giggle,
Beneath trees with mustache-like fronds,
I played peek-a-boo with a turtle,
While a shrimp serenaded the ponds.

The sand was a blanket of butter,
And the sun wore a funny old grin.
We danced with the shadows of palm trees,
And let our adventures begin!

A fish told me secrets of laughter,
With bubbles that tickled my nose.
I tried to catch giggles like fireflies,
But caught only some curious toes.

As twilight wrapped its laughter around,
I toasted a marshmallow moon.
We'll meet in the morning for pancakes,
For a breakfast of joy and a tune!

Lullabies of the Heart's Coast

At dusk the sea hummed a soft song,
Where seagulls wore socks made of cheese.
The stars blinked like children in play,
As I swung in a hammock with ease.

Little fish threw a shindig in tide,
With limbo contests and ice cream trays.
The moon played the banjo so sweet,
While I twirled in my flip-flop ballet.

My heart's coast was covered in giggles,
Balloons floated high on the breeze.
I chased after jokes on the shoreline,
And tripped over sandcastles with ease.

So let's dream of our silly beach nights,
With laughter wrapped tight like a hug.
We'll dance with the crabs and the stars,
In a carnival we set out to tug!

Glimmers of Light on the Lagoon

On a lagoon where the glowworms jiggle,
I found a boat made of jelly and fun.
The fish wore top hats, oh what a sight,
While the ticklish sea crabs spun 'round in the sun.

Moonbeams dipped into my lemonade,
As laughter bounced off lily pad thrones.
I invited a frog for a jelly dance,
While the otters played fetch with my bones.

The breeze told tall tales of the day,
Of pirates who sailed with no sail.
They giggled and wiggled, it's true,
While searching for treasure or a snail.

So here's to our laughter-filled journeys,
With silliness woven through night.
May glimmers of joy fill our hearts,
As we sail past the stars, feeling light!

Embrace of the Sunlit Gale

A dandy breeze gave my hat a chase,
It danced in circles, such a silly race.
I ran like a chicken, flapping my arms,
That wind sure knows how to play with charms.

My drink took flight, oh what a sight,
Rum in the air, taking its height.
The coconut laughed as it tumbled down,
Rolling away, oh such a clown!

Palm trees swayed, giggling without care,
How can a breeze have such a flair?
It tickles my toes, gives my nose a nudge,
Oh gusty companion, I don't hold a grudge!

With every puff, there's laughter in the lane,
Thanks to you, I'll never walk straight again!
The sun beams bright, tickling every face,
The world's a circus, in this funny place.

Currents of Paradise

The waves tumbled in, like puppies at play,
Splashing the sand in a clumsy buffet.
Seagulls squawked, plotting their heist,
Stealing my chips, not once, but thrice!

Sunbathers scattered when the gull swooped low,
With hoots and cackles, they were quite the show.
Sunscreen flopped out, landing with flair,
"Who needs a tan?!" shrieked loud air!

Surfboards bobbed, like ducks on the lake,
Forging a bond, for giggles' sake.
A crab did the cha-cha, right by my toes,
Laughing at me in its fabulous clothes!

With every wave, joy's tide does rise,
Life's a giggle, watch how it flies.
In this paradise where breezes bin,
Laughter lingers; let the fun begin!

Lullaby of the Swaying Trees

Under the palms, I hear them sing,
The trees are gossipers, sharing their bling.
Whispering tales of the monkey brigade,
They chuckle so loud, they'll never fade!

A parrot chimes in, with colors so bold,
Reciting old stories, never getting old.
"Stay away from the fruit, it's wickedly sweet!"
The trees all nodded, with a rustle, oh so neat.

Crickets serenade the sun's lazy fall,
While I laugh softly at the jungle's ball.
Who knew evening could tickle so good?
A comedy show, like I always knew it would!

Balmy whispers cradle the night's embrace,
As I chuckle and sway, in this lively place.
Mother Nature, dear, your jesting spree,
Keeps my spirit dancing, forever carefree!

Secrets in the Coastal Air

From the shore, I hear secrets that squeal,
A crab's wild giggle, oh what a reel!
"Did you see that seagull, it tripped on a wave?"
The whispers tickle me, like a playful knave.

Shells gossip together, clinking in mirth,
Trading bold stories of their sandy birth.
A starfish told me, with a wink and a grin,
"Life's much more fun when you don't wear a fin!"

The breeze came fluttering, full of delight,
It twirled my hair and refused to take flight.
I'd chase it forever, like a game of tag,
The sky held secrets, all tangled and cragged.

The coastal air, so cheeky and bright,
Keeps laughter alive, well into the night.
With each little puff, wisdom it shares,
In this merry land, joy follows and pairs!

Harbor of Whispering Winds

In the harbor, boats sway and dance,
Seagulls laugh, sharing a glance.
Fish jump high, making a splash,
While old sailors tell tales in a flash.

A crab in a suit scuttles by,
Hollering, "Hey, I'm no ordinary guy!"
With a pinch and a wink, he struts with flair,
While everyone shouts, "Just don't go bare!"

Palm trees chime in with the breeze,
Swinging their fronds, oh, what a tease!
They whisper secrets to the seashells near,
"Let's throw a party, it's time for beer!"

As night falls, the lanterns glow,
Dancing shadows put on a show.
Jellyfish in tutus join the fun,
Under the stars, the laughter's begun.

Skylines Touched by Warmth

High above, the pigeons chat,
Deciding who's the grandest cat.
With hats so big and ties so neat,
They strut along the city street.

Sun shines bright, the heat's a blast,
Ice cream drips and children laugh fast.
A raccoon steals a sandwich with glee,
While folks just smile, happy to see.

Clouds shaped like ducks float on high,
Making everyone pause and sigh.
Someone yells, "Now that's a sight!"
As birds misfire in their flight.

The skyline twinkles, the night winds call,
Kites soar high, oh what a brawl!
Serenades from the rooftops play,
As wind gathers dreams and sends them away.

Beneath the Coconut Palms

Beneath the palms, the laughter flows,
Where the sandy floor is cool like snow.
An ant in sunglasses takes a ride,
In a coconut shell, with nothing to hide.

Squirrels wear hats made of leaves,
Planning heists for holiday treats.
Popcorn kernels fly through the air,
While a pelican tries to catch a chair!

The sun beats down but spirits stay bright,
With silly games that stretch through the night.
A limbo contest with a twist,
While crabs practice their dance, none can resist.

As fruit falls down, it's a sweet parade,
With a pineapple crown, it's all homemade.
"Hurry up, don't miss the show!"
Under these palms, there's nothing but glow.

The Shimmering Path of Light

Along the path, flickering bugs,
Wear party hats and give warm hugs.
A snail in a tux is late for the dance,
Shuffling along, he takes a chance.

The breeze hums a tune that's catchy and fun,
As lizards join in, basking in the sun.
"Come join us!" they shout, "Don't wander away!"
While frogs tap their feet, ready to play.

Moonlight winks, casting shadows so long,
While a crab DJ spins a funny song.
The fireflies twirl, a dazzling sight,
As laughter floats up on this whimsical night.

As dawn approaches, the fun won't cease,
With tired smiles, they tuck in for peace.
"Same time next year?" they ask with delight,
On the shimmering path, everything feels right.

The Swaying Shoreline's Melody

On the beach, the sand does dance,
While people chase their sun-kissed chance.
Seagulls squawk, a comic show,
As sunscreen flies, oh what a glow!

The waves come in, they tickle toes,
While crabs march by in tiny rows.
A beach ball flies, a toddler squeals,
As laughter echoes, joy reveals!

Flip-flops flop in silly haste,
A sunburn's badge, oh, what a taste!
With buckets full of dreams and laughs,
We shimmy, shake, and take our paths!

As sunset paints the sky in gold,
We gather tales of fun retold.
Each breeze a giggle, soft and light,
A swaying rhythm, pure delight!

Wanderlust in the Wind

A kite takes flight, what funny sights,
As tots run 'round in pure delights.
The breeze is strong, it tugs at hats,
Oh dear, watch out for slippery mats!

With fruity drinks in hands we stand,
While monkeys play in shifting sand.
The piña colada's frothy wave,
Turns sour faces into brave!

The palm trees sway, they wear a grin,
As sandcastles grow, letting fun in.
A flip and flop, someone takes a fall,
With giggles high, we all recall!

So let the day bring bright chuckles' cheer,
With every gust, we hold dear.
In laughter's breeze, we find our way,
To chase our dreams till break of day!

Surf's Gentle Embrace

The surfboard bobs, a wild ride,
With every wave, we try to hide.
Wipeouts splash into fits of glee,
As gulls join in the jubilee!

A dude named Rick has quite the flair,
With shades so big, he's full of dare.
He catches one but misses three,
And lands to cheers, oh what a spree!

The ocean whispers secret jokes,
As salty waves tease idle folks.
Floating on boards, we wave and shout,
In watery realms, without a doubt!

The sun dips low, the sky ablaze,
In waves of laughter, we pour our praise.
Each tumble brings a story new,
As we toast to fun, a wild brew!

A Drift Through Verdant Valleys

Through jungles thick, we take a swing,
With monkeys chatty, what joy they bring!
A vine swings low, we twist and shout,
In leafy treasures, there's no doubt!

The birds above are quite the jesters,
Singing tunes that dance like lesters.
With every step, we stomp and sway,
In this green maze, we laugh all day!

The insects buzz in comic haste,
While frogs leap by, they've got such taste.
A hiccup here, a tumble there,
In nature's circus, we're without a care!

As twilight falls, the fireflies bloom,
We gather 'round, dispelling gloom.
With tales of whimsy, we unite,
Through verdant joy, we take our flight!

A Serenade to the Setting Sun

The sun dips low, it's time to play,
A dance of shadows at the end of day.
Flip-flops flying, laughter in the air,
We twirl like penguins, full of flair.

Seagulls squawk, they join our tune,
Chasing each other beneath the moon.
With ice cream drips on soggy shorts,
We sing a song of silly retorts.

The waves applaud with a splash and roar,
As we attempt the limbo on the shore.
In sandy pants and sun-kissed skin,
We can't help but laugh at how we spin.

So here's to sunsets that make us grin,
With goofy moments where we all win.
A serenade that echoes bright,
Of merry mischief beneath twilight.

Breeze-kissed Memories on the Coast

A paddleboard tips, oh what a sight,
With uncoordinated movement, it's quite a fright.
Splashing more than gliding, off it goes,
My friends all giggle, striking funny poses.

Seashells crunching beneath our feet,
We play hide-and-seek with each retreat.
Snort-laughter rips through salty air,
There's nothing like memories we all share.

Kites tangled up in a palm tree's grasp,
We pull and tug, but the wind gives a rasp.
Aerial acrobatics, oh what a mess,
Yet we burst into giggles, under stress.

With lemonade spilled on our sandy quest,
Each moment reminds us we're truly blessed.
In the sun's warm embrace, a funny delight,
We turn the ordinary into pure height.

The Lyrical Flow of the Journey

A sailing hat blows right off my head,
Chasing it down, oh what a spread!
My friends all cackle as I take flight,
In pursuit of that hat, it's quite the sight.

Fish are jumping while I lose my snack,
A seagull swoops, eeeek, don't turn your back!
With chips in hand, I take a stance,
Only to slip and do a silly dance.

We're mapping out treasure, or so we think,
But really it's a quest for a drink.
Pirate antics on this sandy shore,
With shouts of "X marks the spot!" and more!

The laughter blends with the ocean's roar,
As we tumble and fumble, who could ask for more?
The journey's a tune, a whimsical show,
In this crazy adventure, we steal the glow.

A Tender Moment in the Heat

Under the sun, we feel the burn,
Ice cream cones melt, oh when will we learn?
Slapping our cheeks as the drips cascade,
We laugh at the chaos our smiles have made.

With water balloons, oh what a blast,
Each launch unexpected, a splash unsurpassed.
Duck and cover, the battle unfolds,
In the humor of summer, our friendship holds.

The hammock sways like a sleepy cat,
But oh no! Our naps are broken in combat.
As seagulls laugh at our sleepy plight,
We hoot and holler, it's pure delight.

Fresh fruit feast, sticky hands galore,
The flavor's divine, and we're begging for more.
In the heat of the day, we laugh and cheer,
For tender moments make our hearts steer.

Beneath the Canopy of Stars

Beneath the twinkling light, a cat did prance,
Chasing shadows in a curious dance.
A crab with sunglasses strolled the beach,
Saying, "Life's a party, if you just reach!"

Laughter bubbled up from the rock,
As a parrot squawked, "What time's the clock?"
It shrugged its wings, then flew away,
With a wink of mischief at the end of the day.

The moon sat grinning from its plush throne,
As sandcastles toppled, not alone.
A seashell chorus sang by the shore,
Saying, "Build us again, we're never a bore!"

With whispers of joy in every breeze,
The stars giggled down from their leafy trees.
Under a blanket of giggles and cheer,
Even the coconuts laughed, "We're all here!"

The Escape in Every Breath

A pineapple wore shades, oh what a sight,
Rolling down the hill with all its might.
A mango in a hammock sipping its drink,
Shouted, "Life's a smoothie, so let's not think!"

The waves tickled toes and danced with glee,
While a coconut cracked jokes, quite free.
"Why did the fruit salad go out for a run?
To toss in the air and bask in the sun!"

Frogs in sombreros jumped to the beat,
They lost their maracas, oh what a feat!
In this fruity fiesta, the laughter did swell,
As everyone sang, "We're doing so well!"

With every deep breath, a chuckle arose,
As the breeze tickled noses, a fun little pose.
Under the sun, what a silly affair,
Even the seashells danced without a care!

A Dance of Ocean Breezes

A jellyfish waltzed in the shimmering tide,
While dolphins cheered from the water's wide side.
"Let's throw a party, and here's our plan:
With bubbles and giggles, we're the best of the clan!"

The sand held secrets of stories untold,
Of crabs with high hats and wise fish so bold.
An octopus spun a tale with flair,
Waving its arms, "Catch me if you dare!"

Pineapples rolled by, freshly laid back,
While sea breezes hummed—a merry old track.
The starfish clapped hands, or was it a joke?
"Whatever, just join us, stop being a bloke!"

Between the tides, laughter arose,
With every new step, joy in our prose.
Underneath frothy waves that tease,
We danced through the whims of our salty seas!

Whispers of the Palms

In the shade of the palms, stories unfold,
With monkeys in hats being quite bold.
A toucan flew by, squawking a rhyme,
"Let's throw a fiesta, it's party time!"

Coconuts rolled in for a game of charades,
While lizards in shades took sunbathing parades.
The breeze went, "Whoosh!" and the leaves played along,

Creating a melody, oh what a song!

Crickets chimed in with their nighttime tune,
Singing to the stars, a silly festoon.
The fireflies danced in a flickering row,
"Join in our fun, and let the good vibes flow!"

Where laughter is found amongst swaying trees,
And the whispers of joy travel on the breeze.
In this leafy haven, let worries disperse,
For in laughter and fun, there's always a universe!

Under the Canopy of Sky

Under a leaf, I dance in shade,
The sun's been warned, the game delayed.
With every breeze, my hat takes flight,
Chasing it down feels just so right.

The coconuts giggle, they don't care,
As monkeys swing with some flair.
Pineapple hats and jokes so loud,
We're a fruity, silly, laughing crowd.

Here a watermelon joke, there a lime,
They all burst out, stealing the rhyme.
With each gust, my flip-flops clack,
On this zany path, there's no turning back.

So let's toast to this vibrant scene,
With piña coladas and jellybeans.
Under the canopy, life's a jest,
In the shade of joy, we're truly blessed.

Gentle Currents of Summer

With every wave, a splash of fun,
Surfboards scream, they've just begun.
Sandy toes and sunburned noses,
Jokes float by like rising roses.

The seagulls steal my sandwich dreams,
Chasing them down with silly screams.
I cast my line for fish to catch,
But maybe a sea shoe is more my match.

A dolphin winks, oh what a tease,
As I flail about, stuck in a breeze.
Flip-flops fly, oh what a sight,
Summer's a party, from day to night.

So here we are, with laughter bright,
Marshmallows roasting, quite the delight.
Gentle currents, laughter weaves,
In this sunny world, we believe.

Serenade of the Ocean's Breath

On the shore where shells converse,
The ocean's tune sings with a verse.
Waves tickle feet like playful sprites,
As crabs dance awkwardly in their rights.

A beach ball bounces, full of glee,
While seagulls squawk, 'Come dance with me!'
Cooler drinks spill, and laughter roars,
With sunscreen wars on sandy floors.

The sun dips low, a golden glow,
And sun hats fly, oh what a show!
With boogie boards and laughter grand,
We'll forever play on this sun-kissed sand.

So heed the call of salty cheer,
Every wave's a giggle, loud and clear.
Let's serenade the ocean's breath,
With jokes and joy until we're out of breath.

Secret Songs of the Lagoon

In hidden nooks where iguanas sway,
The lagoon whispers, come and play.
Frogs croak tunes, a hilarious beat,
As fireflies dance on tiny feet.

Bamboo boats glide with a twist,
"Row, row!" they shout, "You'll get kissed!"
With every splash, laughter's the guide,
As fish join in, they leap with pride.

A turtle hums, "Join the fun,"
As we try to catch a gleaming bun.
The water giggles, ripples speak,
With secrets shared, we take a peek.

So let's dive deep for joy and light,
In our funny haven, hearts are bright.
With secret songs and laughter's ring,
This lagoon's a place where we all sing.

Song of the Distant Isles

In the distance, bananas sway,
A parrot sings, hip-hip-hooray!
The waves chuckle, oh so bold,
While coconuts spill tales untold.

Sandy feet, oh what a sight,
Dancing crabs join in delight.
Palm trees lean to steal the show,
Their hula moves steal all the flow.

Fruits are ripe, but who will share?
The monkeys giggle, don't they care?
Bright umbrellas, oh so grand,
Marking spots for lively bands.

As the sun begins to melt,
Adventures spark with stealthy pelt.
Let's not wait, the fun won't stop,
In this paradise, we hop, hop, hop!

Mirage of the Evening Zephyr

The evening breeze whispers a tune,
As frogs croak under the moon.
Laughter echoes 'neath the stars,
While geckos play tiny guitars.

Wind chimes jingle, streets alive,
With seagulls swooping, taking a dive.
Coconut drinks, straw hats galore,
Everyone's dancing, who could ask for more?

Shells clatter in a playful jam,
Underfoot, a soft shell clam.
Fishy jokes twist in mid-air,
As the breeze pulls on your hair.

Join the fun, don't hesitate,
Catch a wave or dance a gait.
The night is young, let's make a scene,
In this mirage, life's a dream!

Hushed Murmurs Over the Dunes

The dunes whisper secrets low,
Where kangaroos occasionally show.
A taco truck, what a surprise,
With hot salsa, and snacks that mesmerize.

A rabbit hops, shaking his head,
While beach tales spin from the bread.
Giggles rise with sandy feet,
What a delight, oh what a treat!

Seagulls squawk, playing charades,
While kids in pools throw out cool shades.
The sun yawns, ready to sleep,
As dreams of mischief drift and leap.

Murmurs fade like the tide's retreat,
Tomorrow again, we'll be back for the heat.
So let's pack joy, each ounce we'll take,
In the hush of dusk, fresh memories we'll make!

Awakening of Salt-kissed Breezes

Morning breaks with a giggling sound,
As crabs march like royalty, round and round.
Coffee spills from cups too high,
With splashes that make seagulls cry.

The sun peeks with a funny grin,
Inviting all to join in spin.
Flip-flops squeak with every step,
While pelicans practice their prep.

A beach game, oh what a plan,
To toss the balls and chase the tan.
The sun loves to wrap us in beams,
As we daydream, caught in themes.

As salt-kissed breezes whirl and sway,
We savor each playful, sunny day.
Let's laugh aloud in the warm embrace,
As joy and sunshine fill this place!

Hallowed Grounds of Whispering Waters

In a land where breezes tease,
A parrot sings while doing the squeeze,
Fish flip-flop in raucous delight,
As crabs dance sideways, a comical sight.

Palm trees giggle, swaying around,
Lizards play tag on the warm, soft ground,
Seashells gossip with waves in a splash,
While sunbathers joke, 'Don't ruin my stash!'

Monkeys swing low, taking a chance,
Stealing snacks with a cheeky glance,
All nature's joy in a playful spree,
Bringing smiles, just wait and see!

So come, join in for laughter and cheer,
Where the quirks of nature draw you near,
In this vibrant, lively, joyful place,
You'll find humor in every space!

Embracing the Dance of Nature

The breeze brings tales from afar,
Like a lightstep dancer at a bazaar,
Coconuts roll as the laughter flows,
Bumping the tourists, oh how it goes!

Butterflies flutter, their colors ablaze,
Tickling the noses in a bright, funny daze,
Squirrels put on a wild parade,
Stealing snacks, making mischief, unafraid.

Laughter erupts as the waves take a swing,
Nearby, a pelican attempts a new fling,
With a dive and a flap, it aims for a snack,
Only to miss and fall, oh, what a whack!

Nature is silly; it's clear to behold,
In every creature, stories unfold,
So twirl with the trees where the punchlines land,
And embrace this joyous, wild, funny band!

Gentle Reflections through the Leaves

In the shade where the laughter grows,
Frogs serenade with comical croaks,
The breeze giggles as it plays tag,
With the leaves whispering tales, oh what a rag!

A squirrel wears a nut as a hat,
Chasing its buddy, imagine that!
Cackles of joy echo through the trees,
As nature unfolds its silly decrees.

Clouds pass by like fluffy cotton candy,
While beachgoers slip, oh isn't it dandy?
With sun in their eyes, they trip on a shell,
And laughter erupts, like a ringing bell!

Reflections shimmer in giggly streams,
Nature's humor is woven with dreams,
A world of fun where joy reigns supreme,
In this leafy realm, life's a whimsical dream!

Where Dreams and Waters Meet

Under the sun, where ripples prank,
Fish strike poses in their colorful tank,
While surfers crash in the surf's grand play,
A dance of chaos on a warm, bright day.

Seagulls squawk with a cheeky flair,
As they swoop down to steal your pear,
Beach towels flutter as wind has its say,
In this charming circus, come laugh and stay!

Driftwood sculptures with silly grins,
Wave at the people, let the fun begin,
With every splash, a new joke emerges,
Bringing delight as the laughter surges.

At sunset's glow, the mischief won't quit,
Where dreams and waters in humor fit,
Join the ballet of craziness and cheer,
In this merriment, love, and laughter appear!

www.ingramcontent.com/pod-product-compliance
Lightning Source LLC
Chambersburg PA
CBHW072221070526
44585CB00015B/1435